HAMMERED DULCIMER PLAYING

Comprehensive Guide from Beginner to Expert: Explore the Origins, Master Techniques, Embrace Various Styles, Expand Your Collection, and Improve Stage Performance with Pro Tips on Maintenance and Troubleshooting.

SVEN RALF

Copyright © 2025 By Sven Ralf

All Right Reserved

No part of this work may be reproduced, stored in a retrieval system, or transmitted in any form or by any means—whether electronic, mechanical, photocopying, recording, or otherwise—without the prior written permission of the author, except for brief excerpts used in reviews, scholarly analysis, or other instances of legally recognized fair use.

All rights are reserved by the author. For permission requests, licensing inquiries, or concerns regarding rights, please contact the author directly in writing. Unauthorized use or distribution is prohibited and may lead to legal action in accordance with copyright laws.

Published by Sven Ralf

Disclaimer

This book provides general guidance and educational support for learning to play musical instruments. While the techniques and advice can aid in skill development, they are not a substitute for personalized instruction from a qualified music teacher. Progress may vary depending on practice, experience, and correct application of techniques.

The author and publisher make no guarantees regarding the completeness, accuracy, or suitability of the material for every learner. As music education evolves, this book may not reflect the latest teaching methods or research. For personalized advice tailored to your specific goals, challenges, or physical needs, it is recommended to consult a professional instructor.

Safety and Responsibility

Maintaining proper posture, caring for your instrument, and using correct techniques are essential to avoid injury or damage. Always follow safety guidelines provided by certified instructors.

The author and publisher disclaim any liability for harm, loss, or damage—including to instruments, property, or personal well-being—arising from the use or misuse of this book's content. By using this material, you assume full responsibility for your learning experience and agree to prioritize safe and informed practice.

Contents

Inside This Book 9

CHAPTER ONE 13

Introduction 13

Why the Hammered Dulcimer is a Unique and Rewarding Instrument 14

Overview of the Learning Process 17

What to Expect from This Guide 21

CHAPTER TWO 25

Getting Started with the Hammered Dulcimer 25

Understanding the Hammered Dulcimer: Anatomy and Design 26

Choosing the Right Dulcimer for You 28

Proper Tuning and Maintenance of Your Instrument 30

First Steps: Holding the Mallets and Positioning Your Hands 32

Basic Music Theory Essentials for Beginners 34

CHAPTER THREE 37

Basic Techniques for Playing the Hammered Dulcimer 37

Mastering the Mallet Grip 38

Learning the Simple Striking Technique 39
Developing Your Sense of Rhythm...............41
Introduction to Simple Scales and Arpeggios 42
Playing Your First Melodies 44

CHAPTER FOUR 47
Essential Hammered Dulcimer Skills................47
1. Understanding the Role of Both Hands 47
2. Playing in Different Octaves......................49
3. Introduction to Chordal Accompaniment.51
4. Building Speed and Precision in Your Playing 53
5. Techniques for Smooth Transitions Between Notes 54

CHAPTER FIVE 57
Expanding Your Musical Repertoire..................57
Learning Easy Folk Tunes and Melodies 59
Understanding Song Structure: Verses, Choruses, and Bridges...................................61
Introducing Ornamentation: Trills, Rolls, and Grace Notes...64
Exploring Different Styles of Music for Hammered Dulcimer......................................67

CHAPTER SIX 71

Practicing for Progress: Creating Effective Routines 71

The Power of Consistency: How Much Should You Practice? 71

Developing Focus and Avoiding Common Mistakes 74

Using a Metronome to Build Timing and Speed 76

How to Break Down and Master Challenging Pieces 78

Tips for Effective Practice Sessions 80

CHAPTER SEVEN 83

Getting Started with the Hammered Dulcimer 83

Understanding the Hammered Dulcimer: Anatomy and Design 84

Choosing the Right Dulcimer for You 86

Proper Tuning and Maintenance of Your Instrument 88

First Steps: Holding the Mallets and Positioning Your Hands 90

Basic Music Theory Essentials for Beginners 92

Conclusion 95

Reflecting on Your Hammered Dulcimer Journey 96

Continuing to Grow as a Musician: Resources and Next Steps..98

Encouragement to Keep Practicing and Enjoying Your Music....................................100

Final Words of Inspiration..........................102

Inside This Book

From Practice to Performance: The Complete Beginner's Guide to Mastering Music Skills Quickly with Simple Techniques and Proven Methods for Rapid Skill Development is an essential resource for anyone eager to embark on a musical journey, whether you're picking up an instrument for the first time or seeking to refine your foundational skills. This book offers a step-by-step guide to quickly mastering musical techniques, making it an invaluable tool for beginners who are determined to progress from practice to actual performance. The unique approach lies in the simplicity of the methods combined with proven strategies for rapid skill development, allowing readers to experience tangible results in a shorter time frame.

Have you ever wondered how professional musicians seem to glide effortlessly through complex pieces, or how they achieve such mastery? This guide demystifies that process by breaking down key musical skills into manageable, easily digestible segments. With each chapter, you'll be able to apply these skills in your practice sessions and quickly notice improvements. From understanding rhythm and pitch to mastering the art of timing and dynamics, every essential aspect of musicianship is covered. The book invites you to participate actively by applying these strategies, ensuring that you don't just read about improvement, but experience it for yourself.

What makes this book particularly engaging is its focus on actionable learning. Each chapter is designed not only to explain techniques but also to encourage you to put them into practice immediately. As you work through the sections on topics like finger positioning, breathing techniques, and music theory basics, you'll feel more confident in your ability to progress quickly. The methods outlined have been tested and proven by professional musicians and educators, ensuring that you are learning in the most effective way possible.

CHAPTER ONE
Introduction

Welcome to *Hammered Dulcimer Playing*—a journey into the world of one of the most fascinating and ancient musical instruments. Whether you're a seasoned musician or a beginner, the hammered dulcimer offers a unique and enriching experience for those who wish to explore its soothing sounds and diverse musical possibilities.

The hammered dulcimer, with its shimmering tones and distinctive structure, has long been cherished in many cultures worldwide. From its origins in ancient Persia to its place in the folk music of Appalachia, this instrument has crossed time and geography to provide a source of beauty, inspiration, and joy for generations. Learning to play this versatile instrument opens up a new world of musical discovery, one where you can experiment with melodies, harmonies, and rhythms that are both intricate and captivating.

In this guide, you'll find everything you need to begin your journey as a hammered dulcimer player. We'll dive deep into the history, technique, and practical steps to mastering this instrument, offering you a comprehensive roadmap to get you from your first note to your first performance. Whether you plan to play traditional folk tunes, classical pieces, or contemporary compositions, the hammered dulcimer will allow you to express yourself in unique and beautiful ways.

Why the Hammered Dulcimer is a Unique and Rewarding Instrument

The hammered dulcimer stands out in the world of musical instruments for its distinct structure, playing technique, and captivating sound. What makes this instrument so unique and appealing to both beginners and advanced players alike?

A Historical Legacy: The hammered dulcimer has been around for centuries, with early versions of the instrument appearing in ancient civilizations. Its evolution through time has shaped it into the modern form we know today. The dulcimer's widespread popularity across diverse cultures—from European folk music to the Middle Eastern and Asian traditions—adds layers of richness to its sound and style.

The Sound: There's no other instrument quite like the hammered dulcimer when it comes to its tonal quality. The strings, struck by mallets, produce a bright, resonant sound that can be both delicate and powerful. The harmonic overtones generated by the vibrations of the strings give it an ethereal quality that can soothe, uplift, or energize, depending on the style of play.

Versatility: The hammered dulcimer's versatility is another reason it is so rewarding to learn. Whether you prefer playing traditional folk songs, classical music, or experimenting with your own compositions, the hammered dulcimer's layout and structure provide flexibility in both melody and harmony. Its large range of strings offers opportunities for creative expression, while the mallets themselves allow for different dynamic levels, from soft whispers to bright, powerful accents.

Physical Engagement: Unlike instruments such as the piano or violin, which require intricate finger placement, the hammered dulcimer allows you to focus on rhythm and dynamics as much as pitch. The act of striking the strings with mallets engages the whole body, offering an enjoyable physical experience. Playing the hammered dulcimer requires coordination, timing, and precision, but it also fosters a sense of mindfulness and calm, allowing players to immerse themselves fully in the music.

For many, playing the hammered dulcimer becomes more than just an instrument to master—it's a journey into musical expression, emotional depth, and cultural exploration. Whether you're seeking a new hobby or looking to deepen your musical skills, the hammered dulcimer offers a unique path to creativity and joy.

Overview of the Learning Process

Learning to play the hammered dulcimer may seem like a daunting task at first, but with the right approach, it can be a thoroughly rewarding experience. The key to mastering this instrument lies in patience, practice, and understanding its structure and technique. In this section, we'll outline a clear pathway to guide you from a beginner to a skilled player.

Step 1: Getting Acquainted with the Instrument: Your journey begins with understanding the hammered dulcimer itself. The instrument consists of a series of strings stretched across a wooden frame. These strings are tuned in courses (sets of strings tuned to the same pitch) and are struck with two mallets. Getting familiar with the instrument's parts, such as the bridges, dampers, and tuning pegs, will help you understand how sound is produced and what each component's role is.

Step 2: Learning Proper Technique: Once you understand the basics of the instrument's structure, you'll move on to learning proper technique. This involves learning how to hold and strike the mallets, how to navigate the dulcimer's layout, and how to control the dynamics of your play. As you practice, you'll develop muscle memory that will allow you to play more fluidly, with precision and expression. Learning the fundamentals of technique is crucial to developing a strong foundation in dulcimer playing.

Step 3: Mastering Basic Melodies and Chords: With proper technique in place, you'll begin learning simple melodies and basic chord progressions. The hammered dulcimer's layout is similar to a piano, with the strings laid out in a scale-like arrangement. As you begin playing, you'll notice how the proximity of the strings allows for smooth transitions between notes and chords. Learning these building blocks will give you the ability to play simple tunes and build your confidence.

Step 4: Exploring Advanced Techniques: As you become more comfortable with basic playing, you'll be ready to explore more advanced techniques. This may involve playing more complex pieces, learning to play with both hands in different registers, and mastering intricate ornamentations like trills and arpeggios. Advanced techniques will add richness to your playing and allow you to explore different musical genres, such as classical, folk, and even contemporary styles.

Step 5: Performing and Improvising: As you progress, you'll likely feel the desire to perform for others or even improvise your own compositions. Performing is a powerful way to refine your skills and share the beauty of the hammered dulcimer with others. Improvisation, while challenging, is a highly rewarding skill that allows you to express your creativity and inventiveness on the spot. This is the point where you can fully begin to make the hammered dulcimer your own and explore your personal musical voice.

Throughout the learning process, it's important to be patient and consistent. Progress may come slowly at first, but with regular practice and dedication, you will soon see significant improvement. Embrace the process, and remember that every step forward, no matter how small, is a victory.

What to Expect from This Guide

This guide is designed to take you through every step of the process of learning to play the hammered dulcimer—from the very first note to performing confidently in front of an audience. Inside, you'll find detailed lessons, expert tips, and clear instructions to help you along the way.

Comprehensive Coverage: This guide will cover all aspects of hammered dulcimer playing, including instrument setup, tuning, basic techniques, and advanced skills. We'll walk you through the different playing styles and the various musical genres that the hammered dulcimer can handle, from traditional folk music to classical arrangements and beyond.

Practice Exercises: To help you develop your skills, we've included a series of practice exercises tailored to each stage of your learning journey. These exercises are designed to gradually build your technique and understanding of the instrument, ensuring that you progress steadily and confidently.

Performance Tips: Alongside technical instruction, this guide will offer advice on how to prepare for performance. We'll discuss stage presence, how to deal with performance anxiety, and tips for playing in front of others. Performance is a critical part of becoming a well-rounded hammered dulcimer player, and we want you to feel prepared and confident when the time comes.

Learning at Your Own Pace: One of the benefits of learning to play the hammered dulcimer is the flexibility it offers. Whether you prefer to take your time and learn slowly or jump straight into complex pieces, this guide is structured to allow you to progress at your own pace.

An Invitation to Explore: This guide is not just a manual for learning an instrument; it's an invitation to immerse yourself in a rich musical tradition and discover the joy of making music. We encourage you to approach this journey with an open mind, a sense of curiosity, and a willingness to explore the many facets of the hammered dulcimer.

By the end of this guide, you'll have a solid understanding of how to play the hammered dulcimer, and you'll be well on your way to mastering this beautiful and unique instrument. Let the music begin!

CHAPTER TWO
Getting Started with the Hammered Dulcimer

The journey of learning to play the hammered dulcimer begins with understanding the instrument itself. Whether you're a complete beginner or someone with prior musical experience, this ancient and beautiful instrument offers a captivating experience for players of all ages. The hammered dulcimer is distinct in its appearance and the sounds it creates, and starting your musical journey on this instrument can be both fulfilling and inspiring.

The first step in learning how to play the hammered dulcimer is becoming familiar with the instrument's anatomy and function. In this section, we will explore the basics of the hammered dulcimer, its unique features, and how it differs from other stringed instruments.

Understanding the Hammered Dulcimer: Anatomy and Design

The hammered dulcimer is a stringed instrument that originated in the Middle East and later spread across Europe and the Americas. It consists of a large, trapezoidal wooden body with a series of strings stretched across it, typically tuned to diatonic or chromatic scales. The instrument is played by striking the strings with small mallets, hence the name "hammered dulcimer."

The Body and Soundboard

The body of the dulcimer is typically made of hardwoods such as maple, walnut, or spruce. The soundboard is the top part of the instrument that amplifies the vibrations of the strings. It's crucial for the tonal quality of the dulcimer and determines the richness of the sound.

Strings and Bridges

The strings are attached to the instrument's frame and are divided into courses, each of which may consist of two or more strings tuned to the same note. These strings are stretched over bridges that help divide the string length into different pitches. The quality and tension of the strings contribute significantly to the dulcimer's tone and resonance.

Mallets and Striking Points

The mallets used in hammered dulcimer playing are typically small and light, often made of wood or soft rubber. The way the mallet strikes the strings impacts the sound produced—whether it's a light tap for a delicate sound or a strong strike for a bold, resonant note. Understanding how to use the mallets properly is an essential part of playing the hammered dulcimer.

Choosing the Right Dulcimer for You

Before you dive into learning how to play, selecting the right hammered dulcimer is crucial for your musical development. There are various types and models of dulcimers available, and the choice depends on factors such as sound quality, price, and your playing style.

Size and Style

Hammered dulcimers come in different sizes and styles. The most common sizes include 12/11 (12 courses and 11 notes per course) or 15/14, with the number of strings influencing the tonal range of the instrument. Beginners often start with a smaller, simpler model, while more advanced players may opt for a larger, more complex instrument with a greater range of notes.

Wood and Construction Quality

The material used to construct the dulcimer affects its sound quality. Instruments made from hardwoods like cherry or walnut produce a warmer, richer tone. The craftsmanship of the dulcimer also matters—look for a well-built instrument with quality hardware, strong bridges, and carefully calibrated strings for optimal sound production.

Budget Considerations

Prices for hammered dulcimers can vary widely depending on the brand, size, and material. While higher-end dulcimers offer excellent sound quality, there are many affordable options that provide great value for beginners. Be sure to choose an instrument that fits both your budget and your long-term musical goals.

Proper Tuning and Maintenance of Your Instrument

Once you've chosen your hammered dulcimer, it's essential to keep it properly tuned and maintained. This ensures that the instrument remains in top condition and that you can achieve the best possible sound quality while playing.

Tuning Your Dulcimer

The hammered dulcimer is typically tuned in a diatonic scale, but some players also prefer chromatic tunings for more versatility. Standard tuning for a 15/14 dulcimer is usually D-A-D-A or similar, but this can vary based on the instrument. To tune your dulcimer, you'll need an electronic tuner or tuning app that can detect the pitch of each string.

When tuning, always adjust the strings slowly and evenly to avoid over-tightening, which could damage the instrument. Start with the middle strings and work outward, checking the tuning after each adjustment.

Maintaining the Dulcimer

In addition to tuning, your dulcimer will require regular maintenance. Wipe the strings and soundboard with a soft, dry cloth to prevent dust buildup, which can interfere with the sound quality. Check the strings regularly for signs of wear and tear, and replace any broken or worn strings promptly.

The bridges and tuning pins should also be checked periodically. Loose or faulty tuning pins can cause problems with keeping the instrument in tune, so make sure they are secure. If you notice any issues with the structure or sound quality of the dulcimer, take it to a professional for maintenance and repairs.

First Steps: Holding the Mallets and Positioning Your Hands

Your mallet technique and hand positioning are crucial to producing the best sound on your hammered dulcimer. Developing proper habits from the start will make your playing more comfortable and efficient.

Proper Mallet Grip

When you pick up your mallets, ensure that you hold them lightly but firmly, similar to holding a pencil or a paintbrush. Your grip should allow flexibility and control without tension. The mallet should rest comfortably in your hands, with your thumb and index fingers lightly holding it.

Striking the Strings

The way you strike the strings will determine the tonal quality you achieve. When you're first starting, focus on playing with a light touch. Hold the mallet at a slight angle and tap the string gently. Experiment with different mallet positions and find what works best for your playing style.

Hand Positioning

Good hand positioning is essential for both comfort and sound quality. Keep your wrists relaxed, with your arms slightly bent and hovering just above the dulcimer. Avoid reaching too far or tightening your muscles; your arms and hands should move fluidly, using minimal effort.

Basic Music Theory Essentials for Beginners

Before diving into more complex pieces, understanding some basic music theory will help you navigate the world of hammered dulcimer playing with greater ease. Here's a look at some essential music theory concepts every beginner should know.

Notes and Scales

The hammered dulcimer typically follows a diatonic scale, which consists of seven notes (the natural scale). Familiarizing yourself with the notes of the scale—C, D, E, F, G, A, and B—is the foundation of understanding how melodies are structured.

Intervals

Intervals are the distances between two notes. The most basic intervals in Western music are the whole step (or whole tone) and half step (or semitone).

Understanding intervals will allow you to play scales, chords, and melodies with greater ease.

Reading Sheet Music

Learning to read sheet music will be essential as you progress. Start with basic musical notation, such as the treble clef (commonly used for melody lines), and practice identifying notes and rhythms on the staff. Over time, you'll become more comfortable reading both sheet music and tablature specifically for the hammered dulcimer.

Chords and Harmony

Once you're comfortable with single notes, you can start learning how to play chords. Chords are combinations of notes played together and create harmony. On the hammered dulcimer, chords can be played by striking multiple strings simultaneously or in quick succession.

With these foundational concepts, you'll be well on your way to learning how to play the hammered dulcimer.

Taking time to understand the instrument, practicing good technique, and incorporating basic music theory will make your learning experience enjoyable and successful.

CHAPTER THREE

Basic Techniques for Playing the Hammered Dulcimer

Playing the hammered dulcimer is a captivating and rewarding experience, but it requires a solid foundation in technique to truly master the instrument. Whether you are a beginner or an intermediate player, learning the basic techniques is essential for building your skills and enhancing your musical expression. This section will guide you through the essential techniques for playing the hammered dulcimer, helping you progress steadily and confidently.

Mastering the Mallet Grip

The mallet grip is the foundation of your playing technique. A proper grip is crucial for controlling the mallets effectively and producing a clear, resonant sound. Beginners often struggle with their mallet grip, as it can be difficult to know how much pressure to apply or where to hold the mallet. However, mastering the mallet grip will drastically improve your playing and give you the precision needed for various musical styles.

To begin, hold the mallet with a relaxed but firm grip. Your fingers should wrap comfortably around the handle, and your thumb should rest lightly on the side of the mallet, opposite your fingers. This grip should resemble holding a pencil or a drumstick, ensuring that you have control without unnecessary tension in your hand or wrist.

One common mistake is holding the mallet too tightly. Tension will lead to poor sound quality and fatigue. Aim for a relaxed grip, allowing your wrist to be flexible. The mallet should feel as though it is an extension of your arm, moving with ease across the strings. Practice with both mallets in each hand, experimenting with different grips to find the most comfortable and effective hold for you.

Learning the Simple Striking Technique

Striking the strings of the hammered dulcimer properly is one of the most important skills to develop early on. The correct striking technique ensures that you get a clean, sustained sound, with proper articulation and tone.

To strike the strings, use the mallets to tap the strings lightly but firmly. Position the mallet just above the string you want to strike, and avoid letting the mallet "bounce" off the string. A consistent motion is key; rather than flicking the wrist or slamming the mallet down, try to develop a smooth, controlled striking motion. The mallet should strike the strings in a straight line, keeping your wrist relaxed but responsive.

The position of your mallet in relation to the dulcimer's strings is important. Strike the strings near the center, rather than at the ends, to produce a fuller, richer tone. Experiment with different striking positions to understand how this affects the sound. Additionally, varying the force of your strikes will give you more dynamic range in your playing.

As you progress, you will learn to strike multiple strings at once, creating chords or more complex melodies. However, before moving on to these advanced techniques, mastering the simple striking technique is essential to achieving a balanced sound.

Developing Your Sense of Rhythm

Rhythm is one of the most important aspects of music, and developing a solid sense of rhythm will help you play the hammered dulcimer with precision and musicality. The hammered dulcimer is often used in a variety of musical styles, and being able to keep a consistent rhythm will ensure that you play in time with other musicians or with a metronome.

Start by practicing simple rhythmic patterns with a metronome. Begin with quarter notes, eighth notes, and rests, gradually increasing the complexity as you become more comfortable. Use the metronome to help you maintain a steady tempo, and focus on striking the strings at the correct times. Your goal is to keep the rhythm consistent and fluid, without rushing or lagging behind the beat.

Once you feel confident with basic rhythms, try incorporating syncopated rhythms or more complex time signatures. Many pieces of hammered dulcimer music involve intricate rhythmic patterns, so practicing these will improve your ability to adapt to different musical styles.

Listening to music in different time signatures and rhythmic patterns will also help develop your sense of rhythm. By hearing how different rhythms fit together, you'll gain a better understanding of how rhythm shapes the music you play.

Introduction to Simple Scales and Arpeggios

Scales and arpeggios are the building blocks of music. Learning these on the hammered dulcimer will improve your technique and help you gain a deeper understanding of musical structure. Scales provide the foundation for melodies, and arpeggios are essential for playing chord progressions.

Start with a simple major scale. Position your hands over the strings and practice playing one note at a time in ascending and descending order. Focus on evenness and clarity as you play, making sure each note rings out clearly. As you become comfortable with one scale, try different keys or explore minor scales to diversify your playing.

Arpeggios are played by striking the notes of a chord one after another, rather than all at once. Begin by learning the arpeggios of basic major and minor chords. Start slowly, and practice playing each note of the chord in a smooth, flowing manner. The goal is to make the arpeggio sound like a single, connected phrase, rather than a series of individual notes.

Learning scales and arpeggios will not only improve your technical skill but will also help you develop a better ear for harmony and melody. Once you are comfortable with basic scales and arpeggios, you can start to incorporate them into the music you play.

Playing Your First Melodies

Now that you have the basic techniques down, it's time to move on to playing your first melodies. Playing melodies on the hammered dulcimer is one of the most rewarding aspects of learning the instrument, as it allows you to express yourself musically and share beautiful music with others.

Start with simple songs or exercises that use basic rhythms and scale patterns. Focus on playing cleanly, with attention to rhythm and tone. As you become more comfortable with melodies, you can increase the complexity of the pieces you play, incorporating more advanced techniques like finger and hand coordination, ornamentation, and varied dynamics.

When learning melodies, it is important to break down the piece into smaller sections. Practice each section slowly and gradually increase the speed as you gain confidence. Don't rush—mastery takes time, and playing slowly will help ensure accuracy.

As you gain more experience, you can begin to experiment with improvisation, incorporating your own ideas into the music. The hammered dulcimer lends itself beautifully to improvisational playing, allowing for creativity and personal expression. Begin by altering rhythms or embellishing the melody with your own ornaments.

Through consistent practice and a focus on developing your fundamental techniques, you will soon be able to play more complex pieces and enjoy the full range of possibilities the hammered dulcimer offers.

CHAPTER FOUR

Essential Hammered Dulcimer Skills

The hammered dulcimer is a captivating and unique instrument with a rich, resonant sound. It is often described as a bridge between string and percussion instruments, producing beautiful melodies and harmonies. To master the hammered dulcimer, there are a few core skills you must develop. Whether you're a beginner or an intermediate player, focusing on these essential skills will help elevate your playing and allow you to play a wide variety of musical pieces with both precision and emotional expression.

1. Understanding the Role of Both Hands

One of the most important aspects of playing the hammered dulcimer is understanding how to use both hands effectively. Unlike other stringed instruments, where one hand is mainly responsible for producing notes and the other for positioning or finger movement, the dulcimer requires both hands to engage in a dynamic relationship with the strings.

The Right Hand typically holds one or two mallets and is responsible for striking the strings in a controlled yet expressive manner. The mallets should be held loosely, with enough grip to guide them across the strings but without unnecessary tension, which can affect the sound quality.

The Left Hand plays a complementary role. It is often responsible for damping or muting strings after they have been struck, as well as occasionally playing additional notes or chords. The left hand must move with precision and fluidity to prevent unwanted noises or overtones that can muddy the sound.

Working to coordinate both hands is key to producing clean, crisp sounds. As you become comfortable with each hand's role, you'll notice how fluid transitions become, and the distinct layers of sound that your hands can create together.

2. Playing in Different Octaves

Playing in multiple octaves adds depth and variety to your playing, and the hammered dulcimer is well-suited for this because of its vast range. The dulcimer typically spans several octaves, and learning to navigate these octaves effectively is essential for any serious player.

Why Playing in Octaves is Important: Each octave on the hammered dulcimer offers a unique quality of sound. Lower octaves have a rich, full sound, while higher octaves provide a brighter, more shimmering tone. By learning to play across different octaves, you can create more dynamic and expressive melodies. Playing in different octaves also allows for greater flexibility when performing different styles of music, from classical to folk to contemporary.

How to Play in Multiple Octaves: As a beginner, it can be challenging to shift your playing between octaves smoothly. Start by familiarizing yourself with the layout of your dulcimer. The strings are arranged in sets of courses, and each course represents a note in a given octave. To practice octave shifts, start by playing a simple melody in a lower octave and then move it up to the next octave. Focus on maintaining a consistent rhythm and tone quality when transitioning between octaves. Over time, this will become second nature.

3. Introduction to Chordal Accompaniment

In addition to playing melodies, hammered dulcimer players often need to provide chordal accompaniment to support a singer or other instrumentalists. This requires an understanding of harmony and the ability to build chords quickly and accurately.

Understanding Chord Structure: Chords are built from a combination of specific notes that complement the melody. In most Western music, the basic chords are major, minor, diminished, and augmented. Each chord has a specific set of notes associated with it, and you can build them in various voicings across the dulcimer.

How to Play Chords on the Dulcimer: On the hammered dulcimer, chords are played by striking multiple strings simultaneously with the mallets. While it's possible to play these chords in a traditional piano-style fashion, the dulcimer's layout means that you may need to spread your hands out over several different strings to create the chord. Begin by practicing simple triads (three-note chords) in different positions on the dulcimer. Once you've mastered basic triads, work your way to more complex chords, and try incorporating arpeggios (broken chords) into your accompaniment.

Tips for Effective Chordal Accompaniment: Focus on clean, sharp strikes to avoid muddy sounds. Use your left hand to mute unnecessary strings when playing chords. Try using different mallets for different tonal effects—one softer for a mellow sound, and one harder for a more percussive quality. Experiment with rhythmic patterns to match the musical style you're playing.

4. Building Speed and Precision in Your Playing

As with any instrument, speed and precision are vital for becoming a proficient hammered dulcimer player. Speed allows you to play faster musical passages, and precision ensures that your strikes are clean and accurate.

Start Slowly: It's essential to start any new piece slowly and deliberately. This gives you the opportunity to develop muscle memory for each note, chord, and transition. Focus on accuracy before increasing speed. If you're playing a fast passage, try to ensure that each note is clearly articulated and that there's no unnecessary movement.

Gradual Increase in Tempo: Once you've played the piece accurately at a slow tempo, start increasing the speed incrementally. Use a metronome to track your progress. Challenge yourself to push the tempo by small increments rather than jumping straight into an extremely fast tempo.

Practice with Focus: To build both speed and precision, focus on one skill at a time. For instance, if you are struggling with a difficult passage, break it down into smaller segments. Focus on clean strikes, smooth transitions, and hand independence. Once you've nailed a small section, move on to the next one.

5. Techniques for Smooth Transitions Between Notes

Smooth transitions between notes are crucial for maintaining a fluid and pleasant sound. In many ways, how well you transition between notes can make or break the overall quality of your playing.

The Importance of a Relaxed Hand Position: When playing the hammered dulcimer, it's essential to maintain a relaxed hand position. Tension can lead to jerky or abrupt movements between notes, affecting the fluidity of your transitions. Aim for a fluid, controlled motion, allowing your hands to move gracefully across the dulcimer.

Using Legato Techniques: In addition to practicing clean note transitions, it's helpful to incorporate legato playing techniques. Legato playing refers to playing notes smoothly without gaps between them. Practice transitioning from one note to the next with minimal space, and experiment with keeping the mallets on the strings for a more connected sound.

Focus on Finger and Wrist Movements: Pay attention to your wrist and finger movements, as these are the primary factors in smooth transitions. For example, use your wrist to guide the mallet from one note to the next, rather than making jerky, fast movements with your fingers. A smooth wrist motion will create a more fluid sound.

By honing these essential skills, you will not only improve your technical abilities on the hammered dulcimer, but you'll also find yourself more comfortable expressing yourself musically on this beautiful instrument. As you continue to grow as a player, these skills will help you take your playing to new levels, whether you're performing solo or accompanying others.

CHAPTER FIVE
Expanding Your Musical Repertoire

Expanding your musical repertoire on the hammered dulcimer opens up an entire world of possibilities for musical expression. The hammered dulcimer, with its distinct sound and melodic richness, can enhance a variety of genres. By learning new pieces and exploring different styles, you not only grow as a musician but also develop your musical ear and ability to adapt to various musical contexts.

One of the first ways to expand your repertoire is by introducing new genres into your practice. While traditional folk tunes form the core of hammered dulcimer playing, exploring other genres like classical, jazz, and contemporary music will add a new dimension to your playing. Each genre requires a different approach to technique, rhythm, and phrasing. For instance, classical pieces may require more precise finger control and articulation, while jazz might demand improvisational skills.

Additionally, learning pieces from various musical traditions around the world—such as Celtic, Middle Eastern, or Balkan music—can significantly enrich your playing. Each of these traditions uses unique scales, rhythms, and ornamentations that will broaden your musical horizons. By playing a variety of tunes, you will not only become a more versatile player but also deepen your understanding of the nuances within different musical cultures.

The hammered dulcimer's wide range of tones and the ability to sustain melodies make it a perfect instrument for both complex pieces and simple, straightforward tunes. Expanding your repertoire also means being open to playing in different settings, whether it's a solo performance, ensemble playing, or accompanying dancers. The more you expose yourself to various musical forms, the more you'll be able to express your creativity and individuality on the hammered dulcimer.

Learning Easy Folk Tunes and Melodies

Folk tunes and melodies are some of the most accessible and enjoyable pieces to play on the hammered dulcimer. These simple yet beautiful melodies have stood the test of time because they are often easy to learn and rich in emotional depth. For beginners and seasoned players alike, folk music provides a wonderful foundation upon which to build your skills and musical understanding.

When learning folk tunes on the hammered dulcimer, it's important to begin with simple melodies. Start with well-known tunes like "Greensleeves" or "Shady Grove," which often have repetitive and easy-to-follow structures. These tunes typically emphasize simple rhythms and intervals, making them a great starting point for those still becoming familiar with the hammered dulcimer's layout.

As you become more comfortable with the basics, you can challenge yourself by learning more intricate variations of these folk tunes. Many folk melodies are passed down through generations, and each version can bring new elements such as different harmonies, rhythm patterns, or ornamentations. As you explore these variations, you will begin to understand the nuances of playing folk music on the hammered dulcimer and how to interpret the same melody in different ways.

Folk tunes are also excellent for practicing your improvisational skills. The repetitive nature of folk melodies often allows for embellishments, personal interpretations, and flourishes. In folk music, improvisation is not just about changing the melody; it's about adding your own voice to the tradition. Experiment with changing the rhythm or adding harmonies to transform a basic melody into something uniquely yours.

Moreover, learning folk tunes will help you develop your musical ear. These songs often feature simple chord progressions and predictable melodies, making them an ideal training ground for hearing intervals and understanding how notes relate to each other. As you progress, you can learn to incorporate more complex techniques into these folk tunes, helping you to play with greater expression and creativity.

Understanding Song Structure: Verses, Choruses, and Bridges

One of the keys to becoming a proficient hammered dulcimer player is understanding song structure. Knowing how to navigate the sections of a song—such as verses, choruses, and bridges—will help you organize your playing and add depth to your musical interpretations. Whether you're playing a traditional folk song or a modern tune, recognizing these elements will allow you to build your performance and captivate your audience.

The **verse** of a song typically sets up the main story or theme. It is the part that you repeat several times with slight variations, and it usually carries the melody. On the hammered dulcimer, playing the verses means establishing the song's identity, whether it's through a straightforward melody or a more complex arrangement. The key to playing verses well is to ensure clarity and simplicity, giving the melody room to shine.

The **chorus**, on the other hand, is the part of the song that often carries the emotional or thematic weight. It is usually more dynamic and can feature a change in harmony or rhythm. When playing the chorus on the hammered dulcimer, it's important to increase the intensity or add more movement, whether through faster rhythms or more ornamented phrasing. This is the part where you can experiment with embellishments or even slight variations in the melody to bring out the emotional core of the song.

The **bridge** is the section that provides contrast. It may introduce a new chord progression or shift the song into a different key. It's important to approach the bridge with a sense of surprise or contrast, as it provides a break from the repetition of the verses and choruses. On the hammered dulcimer, playing the bridge can involve shifting to a new register, playing with dynamics, or altering your rhythm patterns to highlight the change in the song's structure.

Understanding these components allows you to add nuance to your performance. For example, knowing when to emphasize the verses and when to build up to the chorus will make your playing more dynamic and engaging. Additionally, it will help you decide when to hold back and when to unleash the full potential of the hammered dulcimer, ensuring that each section of the song has its moment to shine.

Introducing Ornamentation: Trills, Rolls, and Grace Notes

Ornamentation is what makes the hammered dulcimer a particularly expressive instrument. Trills, rolls, and grace notes are essential tools for adding complexity, depth, and beauty to your playing.

These subtle decorations are not just flourishes—they can completely transform a simple melody into something captivating.

Trills involve rapidly alternating between two notes, typically a step apart. On the hammered dulcimer, trills can be a stunning way to add ornamentation to any piece. By practicing controlled trills, you can develop greater finger independence and dexterity. When executed correctly, trills can evoke a sense of urgency or tension, depending on their placement in the song. For example, a trill before a major melodic shift can heighten anticipation and draw attention to the upcoming change.

Rolls are another form of ornamentation where you rapidly strike several notes in succession, creating a flowing, sustained sound. Rolls are particularly effective in bringing out the resonance of the hammered dulcimer and adding a dreamy, ethereal quality to the music. They can be used in both fast-paced tunes and slower, more contemplative pieces. Mastering rolls allows you to play more fluidly, smoothing over transitions between notes and phrases while adding richness to the texture of the music.

Grace notes are quick, ornamenting notes that are played just before the main note of a melody. They're typically played so quickly that they don't disrupt the primary rhythm or melody but rather enhance it. Grace notes are often used to add subtle embellishments that draw the ear's attention to specific notes. For example, adding a grace note before a strong downbeat can create a slight delay that adds drama or surprise to the melody. Practicing grace notes requires good timing and the ability to strike the hammered dulcimer with precision and control.

Each form of ornamentation has its place in hammered dulcimer music. The key to using them effectively is moderation and knowing when and where to add them. Too many ornaments can clutter the music and distract from the melody, while too few may make the piece feel too plain. With practice, you'll learn how to strike a balance, using ornamentation to elevate the music without overwhelming it.

Exploring Different Styles of Music for Hammered Dulcimer

The hammered dulcimer is an incredibly versatile instrument capable of fitting into many different musical styles. By exploring a range of genres, you'll gain new insights into your instrument and its potential. Let's take a look at some popular styles you can experiment with.

Traditional Folk Music: This is the heart of hammered dulcimer playing. Folk music often features simple melodies and harmonies, making it an ideal genre for beginners. The dulcimer's melodic and harmonic capabilities lend themselves well to the storytelling aspect of folk music, and many folk tunes have been passed down for generations. Mastering this style will give you a solid foundation and an appreciation for the history of the instrument.

Celtic Music: Known for its rhythmic drive and emotional depth, Celtic music is a natural fit for the hammered dulcimer. The fast-paced jigs and reels, as well as the slower ballads, require strong rhythmic skills and the ability to execute rapid, articulate movements. Adding ornamentation such as grace notes, rolls, and trills is especially common in this genre, which enhances the melodic lines.

Classical Music: While the hammered dulcimer is not traditionally used in classical music, its unique timbre can lend itself beautifully to this style.

Classical music demands a high level of technical skill and musicality, but it also offers the opportunity to experiment with complex harmonies and counterpoint. By learning classical pieces, you'll challenge your dexterity and expand your understanding of musical form and expression.

Jazz and Improvisation: Jazz presents an exciting challenge for hammered dulcimer players. The freedom of improvisation allows you to break away from strict melodies and experiment with different rhythms and harmonies. Jazz on the hammered dulcimer can blend traditional elements with contemporary techniques, allowing for unique interpretations of standard jazz tunes.

World Music: Many cultures use similar instruments to the hammered dulcimer, such as the santur in Persian music or the yangqin in Chinese music. By exploring these diverse traditions, you can incorporate new scales, rhythms, and ornamentations into your playing. World music broadens your musical vocabulary and opens up opportunities for collaboration with musicians from different cultures.

The hammered dulcimer is a tool for musical exploration, and its sound can be molded to fit into almost any musical style. By challenging yourself to step outside of your comfort zone and explore various genres, you will become a more versatile and skilled player.

CHAPTER SIX
Practicing for Progress: Creating Effective Routines

The journey to mastering the hammered dulcimer is both exciting and demanding, and a solid practice routine is the foundation of progress. Without a structured plan, you may find yourself practicing endlessly without seeing significant improvement. Establishing a practice routine that focuses on various skills while maintaining variety and engagement is essential for steady development.

The Power of Consistency: How Much Should You Practice?

Consistency is one of the most crucial elements of becoming a proficient hammered dulcimer player. Regular practice not only strengthens muscle memory but also enhances your musical intuition, allowing you to progress faster and more effectively. But how much practice is necessary to make noticeable progress?

The Optimal Practice Time

A common misconception is that the more time you spend practicing, the better you will become. In reality, quality trumps quantity. Aim to practice at least 30 minutes to an hour daily, depending on your schedule and goals. Regular practice, even if it's brief, is more effective than occasional marathon sessions. Consistent practice fosters skill retention and the development of subtle nuances that improve your overall musicianship.

Focused Practice vs. Time Spent Playing

It's not about how many hours you put in, but how effectively you use that time. Focused practice, which targets specific skills, is more productive than aimlessly playing through songs. Spend part of your practice working on your weak areas, whether it's technique, timing, or learning new pieces. As you build these skills, your overall playing will improve.

Avoiding Burnout

Practicing consistently is important, but it's also vital to give your mind and body adequate rest. Over-practicing can lead to burnout and physical strain. It's better to have shorter, more focused sessions every day than long, exhaustive sessions that leave you feeling frustrated or fatigued. Incorporate rest and relaxation to avoid mental and physical exhaustion, keeping your practice enjoyable and sustainable.

Developing Focus and Avoiding Common Mistakes

Focus is a cornerstone of effective practice. Many players unknowingly develop bad habits that can hinder progress. One key to growth on the hammered dulcimer is maintaining awareness during your practice, identifying mistakes early, and correcting them before they become ingrained.

Staying Focused During Practice

Distractions can quickly derail a practice session. Ensure you are in an environment free of interruptions, with your instrument easily accessible and ready to go. If you find your mind wandering, take short breaks to reset. Mindful practice—where you're actively paying attention to your posture, technique, and sound—will yield better results than mindlessly going through the motions.

Identifying and Correcting Common Mistakes

Many beginners develop habits such as poor hand positioning, incorrect finger placement, or failing to maintain a steady rhythm. These mistakes may seem harmless at first but can become deeply ingrained if not addressed. Regularly check your technique in front of a mirror or record your practice to identify areas for improvement. Don't hesitate to slow down, simplify a difficult section, and focus on perfecting it before moving on.

Embracing Mistakes as Learning Opportunities

Mistakes are an inevitable part of the learning process. Rather than getting discouraged, view each mistake as an opportunity to grow. If you stumble over a challenging part, slow down and break it down into smaller sections. Mistakes provide valuable insights into areas where you need improvement, so use them as stepping stones toward mastery.

Using a Metronome to Build Timing and Speed

The hammered dulcimer is an instrument where precise timing and rhythm are crucial. Using a metronome can help you develop these skills by keeping you grounded and ensuring your playing is in sync with the beat.

The Importance of Timing

Timing is one of the most challenging aspects for beginners, but it's essential for playing in any musical ensemble or performance. A metronome serves as a constant reminder to stay in time, particularly when you're practicing new pieces or tricky rhythms. It helps you play more confidently and keeps you from rushing or dragging through sections.

Building Speed with Precision

While it's tempting to increase speed too quickly, it's important to build it gradually. Start with a slow tempo and focus on accuracy and smoothness. As you become comfortable, slowly increase the tempo, ensuring that your timing and control remain intact. This controlled approach to speed will allow you to perform faster sections with greater confidence and fewer mistakes.

Varying Your Metronome Practice

Try using your metronome in various ways to challenge yourself. For example, practice at different time signatures, or accentuate certain beats within a measure. These variations will expand your timing skills and deepen your understanding of rhythmic structures, which is vital for playing the hammered dulcimer with musicality.

How to Break Down and Master Challenging Pieces

One of the most satisfying aspects of playing the hammered dulcimer is conquering challenging pieces. However, attempting to play a difficult piece from start to finish can be overwhelming and frustrating. Breaking it down into manageable sections makes the process far more effective and enjoyable.

Divide the Piece into Sections

Start by identifying the most challenging parts of the piece and break them down into smaller, more manageable sections. You don't need to tackle the whole song at once. Focus on one phrase, one measure, or even one set of notes until you have it down pat. Once you feel confident with one section, move on to the next.

Work on Technique Before Speed

Before attempting to play a complex piece at full speed, slow it down and work on your technique. Pay attention to every detail—whether it's finger placement, timing, or articulation. This attention to detail will make it easier to build up speed gradually, and you'll perform the piece with more precision and musicality.

Combine Sections Slowly

Once you have each section mastered, begin combining them. Start with the first two sections, play them slowly and deliberately, and then gradually add more sections. This incremental approach helps you retain the music and makes the piece feel less daunting. Patience is key when working on difficult music, and the effort will be reflected in your performance.

Tips for Effective Practice Sessions

Maximizing the effectiveness of your practice sessions comes down to staying focused, organized, and intentional. Here are some tips to help you get the most out of every practice:

Set a Clear Goal for Each Session

Before you start practicing, decide on a clear objective. Whether it's learning a new song, improving technique, or mastering a particular rhythm, knowing what you want to accomplish will help you stay focused. It's better to complete one task well than to jump around between multiple tasks without making significant progress.

Warm Up Properly

Just like any other physical activity, warming up is essential for effective practice. Start with basic exercises, such as scales or simple chord progressions, to get your fingers moving and your body in sync with the instrument. A proper warm-up prevents injury and helps you play more smoothly during the rest of your practice.

Track Your Progress

Keep a practice journal or make notes about what you worked on and what needs improvement. This allows you to track your progress over time, ensuring that you're moving forward and staying on course. It also gives you a sense of accomplishment as you reflect on how much you've learned.

Incorporate Variety in Your Sessions

While consistency is essential, don't forget to add variety to your practice. Explore new songs, experiment with different rhythms, or try improvising. This variety keeps practice fun and prevents monotony, which helps maintain motivation. Also, it ensures that you develop a well-rounded skill set.

By following these tips, you'll enhance your practice sessions and keep progressing toward mastery of the hammered dulcimer.

CHAPTER SEVEN

Getting Started with the Hammered Dulcimer

The journey of learning to play the hammered dulcimer begins with understanding the instrument itself. Whether you're a complete beginner or someone with prior musical experience, this ancient and beautiful instrument offers a captivating experience for players of all ages. The hammered dulcimer is distinct in its appearance and the sounds it creates, and starting your musical journey on this instrument can be both fulfilling and inspiring.

The first step in learning how to play the hammered dulcimer is becoming familiar with the instrument's anatomy and function. In this section, we will explore the basics of the hammered dulcimer, its unique features, and how it differs from other stringed instruments.

Understanding the Hammered Dulcimer: Anatomy and Design

The hammered dulcimer is a stringed instrument that originated in the Middle East and later spread across Europe and the Americas. It consists of a large, trapezoidal wooden body with a series of strings stretched across it, typically tuned to diatonic or chromatic scales. The instrument is played by striking the strings with small mallets, hence the name "hammered dulcimer."

The Body and Soundboard

The body of the dulcimer is typically made of hardwoods such as maple, walnut, or spruce. The soundboard is the top part of the instrument that amplifies the vibrations of the strings. It's crucial for the tonal quality of the dulcimer and determines the richness of the sound.

Strings and Bridges

The strings are attached to the instrument's frame and are divided into courses, each of which may consist of two or more strings tuned to the same note. These strings are stretched over bridges that help divide the string length into different pitches. The quality and tension of the strings contribute significantly to the dulcimer's tone and resonance.

Mallets and Striking Points

The mallets used in hammered dulcimer playing are typically small and light, often made of wood or soft rubber. The way the mallet strikes the strings impacts the sound produced—whether it's a light tap for a delicate sound or a strong strike for a bold, resonant note. Understanding how to use the mallets properly is an essential part of playing the hammered dulcimer.

Choosing the Right Dulcimer for You

Before you dive into learning how to play, selecting the right hammered dulcimer is crucial for your musical development. There are various types and models of dulcimers available, and the choice depends on factors such as sound quality, price, and your playing style.

Size and Style

Hammered dulcimers come in different sizes and styles. The most common sizes include 12/11 (12 courses and 11 notes per course) or 15/14, with the number of strings influencing the tonal range of the instrument. Beginners often start with a smaller, simpler model, while more advanced players may opt for a larger, more complex instrument with a greater range of notes.

Wood and Construction Quality

The material used to construct the dulcimer affects its sound quality. Instruments made from hardwoods like cherry or walnut produce a warmer, richer tone. The craftsmanship of the dulcimer also matters—look for a well-built instrument with quality hardware, strong bridges, and carefully calibrated strings for optimal sound production.

Budget Considerations

Prices for hammered dulcimers can vary widely depending on the brand, size, and material. While higher-end dulcimers offer excellent sound quality, there are many affordable options that provide great value for beginners. Be sure to choose an instrument that fits both your budget and your long-term musical goals.

Proper Tuning and Maintenance of Your Instrument

Once you've chosen your hammered dulcimer, it's essential to keep it properly tuned and maintained. This ensures that the instrument remains in top condition and that you can achieve the best possible sound quality while playing.

Tuning Your Dulcimer

The hammered dulcimer is typically tuned in a diatonic scale, but some players also prefer chromatic tunings for more versatility. Standard tuning for a 15/14 dulcimer is usually D-A-D-A or similar, but this can vary based on the instrument. To tune your dulcimer, you'll need an electronic tuner or tuning app that can detect the pitch of each string.

When tuning, always adjust the strings slowly and evenly to avoid over-tightening, which could damage the instrument. Start with the middle strings and work outward, checking the tuning after each adjustment.

Maintaining the Dulcimer

In addition to tuning, your dulcimer will require regular maintenance. Wipe the strings and soundboard with a soft, dry cloth to prevent dust buildup, which can interfere with the sound quality. Check the strings regularly for signs of wear and tear, and replace any broken or worn strings promptly.

The bridges and tuning pins should also be checked periodically. Loose or faulty tuning pins can cause problems with keeping the instrument in tune, so make sure they are secure. If you notice any issues with the structure or sound quality of the dulcimer, take it to a professional for maintenance and repairs.

First Steps: Holding the Mallets and Positioning Your Hands

Your mallet technique and hand positioning are crucial to producing the best sound on your hammered dulcimer. Developing proper habits from the start will make your playing more comfortable and efficient.

Proper Mallet Grip

When you pick up your mallets, ensure that you hold them lightly but firmly, similar to holding a pencil or a paintbrush. Your grip should allow flexibility and control without tension. The mallet should rest comfortably in your hands, with your thumb and index fingers lightly holding it.

Striking the Strings

The way you strike the strings will determine the tonal quality you achieve. When you're first starting, focus on playing with a light touch. Hold the mallet at a slight angle and tap the string gently. Experiment with different mallet positions and find what works best for your playing style.

Hand Positioning

Good hand positioning is essential for both comfort and sound quality. Keep your wrists relaxed, with your arms slightly bent and hovering just above the dulcimer. Avoid reaching too far or tightening your muscles; your arms and hands should move fluidly, using minimal effort.

Basic Music Theory Essentials for Beginners

Before diving into more complex pieces, understanding some basic music theory will help you navigate the world of hammered dulcimer playing with greater ease. Here's a look at some essential music theory concepts every beginner should know.

Notes and Scales

The hammered dulcimer typically follows a diatonic scale, which consists of seven notes (the natural scale). Familiarizing yourself with the notes of the scale—C, D, E, F, G, A, and B—is the foundation of understanding how melodies are structured.

Intervals

Intervals are the distances between two notes. The most basic intervals in Western music are the whole step (or whole tone) and half step (or semitone).

Understanding intervals will allow you to play scales, chords, and melodies with greater ease.

Reading Sheet Music

Learning to read sheet music will be essential as you progress. Start with basic musical notation, such as the treble clef (commonly used for melody lines), and practice identifying notes and rhythms on the staff. Over time, you'll become more comfortable reading both sheet music and tablature specifically for the hammered dulcimer.

Chords and Harmony

Once you're comfortable with single notes, you can start learning how to play chords. Chords are combinations of notes played together and create harmony. On the hammered dulcimer, chords can be played by striking multiple strings simultaneously or in quick succession.

With these foundational concepts, you'll be well on your way to learning how to play the hammered dulcimer.

Taking time to understand the instrument, practicing good technique, and incorporating basic music theory will make your learning experience enjoyable and successful.

Conclusion

The journey of mastering the hammered dulcimer is one of constant growth, challenge, and reward. Whether you've just started or are an experienced player, each note played on the dulcimer brings you closer to unlocking its full potential. This beautiful instrument has the power to convey deep emotion, and as you continue your exploration, you'll discover that the dulcimer can serve as both a personal outlet and a form of artistic expression.

Reflecting on your progress is an important part of any musical journey. Look back on how much you've learned, the songs you've played, and the skills you've honed. Perhaps you started with just the basic strokes and simple tunes, but now you find yourself exploring more complex rhythms and melodies. Each step is a testament to your dedication and love for music. Embrace the joy that the hammered dulcimer has brought into your life, and remember that there is always room for improvement and discovery, no matter where you are in your musical path.

Reflecting on Your Hammered Dulcimer Journey

As you reflect on your hammered dulcimer journey, it's important to recognize the growth and dedication it has taken to get to this point. The hammered dulcimer is an instrument that rewards patience, and over time, you've likely encountered both triumphs and challenges. Celebrate those moments when a difficult technique clicked, or when a new piece of music came together after hours of practice. These milestones are what make your musical journey uniquely yours.

It's natural to have ups and downs as a musician. At times, you might feel like progress is slow, but rest assured that every practice session, no matter how small, contributes to your improvement. Reflect on your achievements, no matter how big or small, and be proud of the progress you've made. Perhaps you've overcome technical challenges like mastering new hand movements or adapting to different tuning systems. Recognize these achievements as significant steps toward becoming a more skilled player.

The hammered dulcimer is an instrument that teaches you patience and perseverance. It requires a balance between technique and artistry. As you continue to play, you may discover new layers of complexity in your performances, and that's part of the beauty of the instrument. It invites you to dive deeper and refine your sound, making every musical experience richer than the last.

Continuing to Grow as a Musician: Resources and Next Steps

Musical growth doesn't stop once you've learned the basics. There is always more to explore, and the world of hammered dulcimer music offers a wealth of resources to aid in your continued development. First, think about taking your skills to the next level. This might involve seeking out advanced tutorials, enrolling in workshops, or collaborating with other musicians. The Internet is full of free and paid resources that can help you deepen your understanding of techniques, styles, and the history of the hammered dulcimer.

For those who want a more structured approach, private lessons from a skilled dulcimer teacher can be incredibly beneficial. A teacher can provide personalized feedback and guidance, helping you to refine your technique and explore areas that you may not have considered on your own. Working with someone who has experience can also inspire you to push past creative or technical blocks you may encounter.

Attending hammered dulcimer festivals and events is another excellent way to continue growing as a musician. These gatherings often feature performances, workshops, and jam sessions where you can learn from others, network with like-minded musicians, and even share your own music. By immersing yourself in a community of dulcimer players, you'll gain new perspectives on your playing and find inspiration to keep growing.

Don't forget to make time for listening and analyzing music from other dulcimer players. This helps you understand different interpretations and arrangements, giving you ideas for your own performances. The hammered dulcimer is a versatile instrument, so exploring different genres, from folk to classical to contemporary, can expand your repertoire and playing style.

Encouragement to Keep Practicing and Enjoying Your Music

The key to becoming proficient on the hammered dulcimer is consistent practice. It's tempting to feel discouraged when you face difficulties, but it's important to keep pushing forward. Remember, every moment you spend with your instrument is an investment in your musical future. The process of practicing is where the magic happens—it's where you refine your technique, experiment with new ideas, and discover new ways to express yourself.

Enjoy the process of learning. While it's easy to become focused on perfection, let yourself enjoy the music along the way. The hammered dulcimer, with its rich, resonant tones, invites you to immerse yourself fully in the sound. Take time to savor each melody and let the music flow through you. When you practice, don't just focus on hitting the right notes—feel the rhythm, the energy, and the emotional depth that each piece brings.

Whether you are playing a simple folk tune or a complex classical arrangement, let every practice session be a celebration of your love for the hammered dulcimer. Don't rush the process—let each practice session be its own reward. The more you practice, the more you'll notice improvements, and the more fulfilling your musical journey will become. Enjoy the small victories, like perfecting a tricky passage or finally getting the timing just right. These are the moments that make the journey worthwhile.

Final Words of Inspiration

The hammered dulcimer is not just an instrument; it's a vessel for creativity, expression, and connection. No matter where you are in your musical journey, never forget the power of music to bring joy, healing, and understanding. As you continue to grow as a musician, keep nurturing your passion for the hammered dulcimer. Whether you play for yourself, share your music with others, or perform in front of an audience, remember that your unique voice is something the world deserves to hear.

Embrace challenges as opportunities to learn. Don't be afraid to make mistakes—each one is a stepping stone toward mastery. Keep pushing your boundaries and experimenting with new techniques and sounds. Your musical journey is your own, and there is no wrong way to play. Your passion for the hammered dulcimer is your guide, and it will lead you to places you never imagined.

As you move forward, keep practicing, keep exploring, and most importantly, keep enjoying the music. The hammered dulcimer has endless possibilities, and you are just scratching the surface. May the music you create with your hammered dulcimer fill your life with joy and inspire others along the way.

Made in the USA
Monee, IL
06 May 2025